MEN-AT-ARMS SERIES

EDITOR: MARTIN WINDROW

# Italian Medieval Armies 1300-1500

*Text by* DAVID NICOLLE, Ph.D

*Colour plates by* G. A. EMBLETON

OSPREY PUBLISHING LONDON

Published in 1983 by
Osprey Publishing Ltd
Member company of the George Philip Group
12–14 Long Acre, London WC2E 9LP
© Copyright 1983 Osprey Publishing Ltd
Reprinted 1983, 1985, 1986, 1987

*British Library Cataloguing in Publication Data*

Nicolle, David
    Italian medieval armies, 1300–1500.
    —(Men-at-Arms series; 136)
    1. Armies—Italy—History—1268–1492
    I. Title          II. Series
    355'.00945          U37

    ISBN 0-85045-477-8


Filmset in Great Britain
Printed in Hong Kong

# Introduction

Mercenaries were a common feature throughout most of Europe in the 14th and 15th centuries, and had been known far earlier. But nowhere did such a sophisticated system of hiring, payment and organisation of mercenaries develop as it did in Italy.

This was, of course, a result of the peninsula's special political, economic and social conditions. Here was a region divided into numerous independent or quasi-independent states, but which was also highly urbanised and economically developed. Feudalism had never really taken root, except in the south and in some peripheral areas of the far north. Urban militias in which the poor provided the infantry and the rich the cavalry had, throughout the early Middle Ages, generally been led by a town-based aristocracy. These forces had already re-established the towns' dominance over the countryside, and had preserved Italy from domination by the Holy Roman Emperor and his German armies. The countryside did provide military levies, and was liberally dotted with castles; but in general these fortifications were either dependent upon nearby towns, for whom the surrounding landscape formed a food-producing *contado*, or were owned by local lords who themselves spent most of their lives in town.

The importance of the mercenary rose, either as urban militias declined in military effectiveness; or as political aggressiveness led to a need for standing armies; or as political tensions within the towns became painfully reflected in their militias. It was less true that rising incomes encouraged townsmen to hire others to fulfil their military obligations, or that towns fell under the domination of tyrants who did not trust their turbulent subjects. Many of these phenomena were seen elsewhere in Europe, and similarly led to a greater reliance on mercenaries. Yet Italy remained an extreme case, and the *condottiere*—whose name came from the *condotta* or contract between himself and his employer—was the result.

Whether commander or humble trooper, the condottiere was a complete professional. His skill has never been doubted, but his loyalty and dedication to a particular cause often has. The Italian condottiere's poor reputation was, ironically enough, a result of later criticism within Italy itself. Machiavelli was not the only 16th century propagandist who, harshly judging the political scene in his native land, went on to provide an overstated armchair-strategist's critique of the condottiere system. While a mercenary was obviously not looking for a hero's grave, he was at

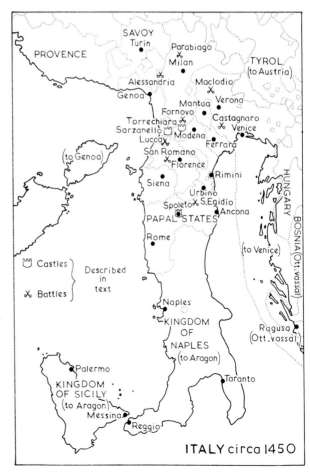

ITALY circa 1450

foreign invasion early in the 16th century may also be less of a condemnation of the condottieri and more a result of changing patterns of warfare. The second half of the 15th century had seen, in France, Spain and elsewhere, the appearance of much larger and to some extent truly national armies, as well as a greater emphasis on gunpowder. Social and economic conditions were also changing rapidly. In fragmented Italy the medieval mercenary leadership became irrelevant or at least changed itself into something else—perhaps eventually into that later officer class which had its roots in much the same minor aristocratic strata. Meanwhile the humble soldier remained, gratefully accepting his pay from a new master.

'The Martyrdom and Glorification of St. James', detail of a late 13th century panel by Andrea di Jacopo d'Ognabene, on the antipendium of the Pistoia Cathedral silver altar. These infantrymen betray some of the Byzantine influences still seen in Italian equipment. One also wears a form of framed war-hat, descended from a late-Roman prototype, which had been in widespread use during the Carolingian era.

the same time a businessman whose livelihood depended on a fair reputation and adequate results.

Various modern historians have done much to set the record straight, among them Michael Mallett, *Mercenaries and their Masters* (London 1974); Geoffrey Trease, *The Condottieri* (London, 1970); and Joseph Deiss, *Captains of Fortune* (London, 1966). The fact that this system persisted for so long must indicate some measure of success. Certainly it would appear that warfare in later medieval Italy—an area of astonishing social, economic, political and even religious tensions—was generally less destructive than in many other parts of Europe. The failure of the system against

# Medieval Mercenaries

Mercenaries had long played an important role in Italian warfare, although during the 12th and 13th centuries local militia remained far more important. The tradition of universal male military service, established by the Lombards in the 8th century, survived in many regions, particularly in the northern and central cities. This was extended to the countryside as towns established their control over their surrounding *contado*. In practice, only the privileged and politically active classes actually bore arms. Militias were organised around city quarters and subordinate towns, while service was normally defensive and rarely lasted more than a week. This, and the local pride so characteristic of medieval Italy, meant that militia service was rarely resented.

Most militiamen were infantry, as few citizens could afford a horse, and the infantryman's skills were, in any case, less specialised than those of the horseman. Wealthier militia cavalry often tended to come from the rural petty-nobility. In open battle, as in the manning of their city walls, the infantry had a primarily defensive role, at least until the crossbow was widely adopted. Lacking much training, but with plenty of determination and numbers, they formed a screen from which their cavalry could make its charges. Meanwhile the *carroccio*, a cart bedecked with the city's standards, provided a focal point and command-post for the entire army.

Given Italy's commercial and military role in the Crusades, it is not surprising that Muslim archery was soon reflected in Italian equipment and tactics. The growing importance of archery, particularly of the crossbow, and the consequently increasing weight of body armour for horsemen and of shields for infantry, was one fundamental reason why professionals took over so much of the fighting. Genoa and Pisa, which had close commercial contacts with the eastern Mediterranean, produced Italy's first specialist crossbowmen, while it is worth noting that the composite bow of Byzantine form had, in fact, never been abandoned in medieval Italy.

Many other infantry now put aside sword, buckler and short spear in favour of a long pike and the large mantlet, probably of Persian origin, held by a shield-bearer. Horsemen meanwhile adopted increasing amounts of plate armour, plus horse-armour and spare mounts, all entailing greater expense and training. Herein lay the origins of the 'lance', the smallest cavalry unit which, by its very nature, tended to be professional and mercenary.

While political circumstances led employers to favour foreigners, these could as well be Italians from another city as men from beyond the Alps. At first few in number, they were recruited individually. As the 13th century progressed mercenary units became permanent features in some cities, though their membership might well fluctuate. Mercenaries were soon being enlisted in small ready-formed groups under their own leadership. Many had come to Italy as part of Imperial or Angevin armies while others, hearing of the opportunities, arrived on their own. During

**An effigy of an Angevin nobleman of the Kingdom of Naples, 1300–1325, in Salerno Cathedral. It is identical in all but detail to the supposed effigy of Charles II, king of Naples and Sicily, in Lucera Cathedral. His hardened leather leg and arm defences (note patterning) and his cuirass are typically Italian.**

The ruined fortress of Gerace stands on a crag overlooking the vital road along the eastern coast of Calabria. It retains much of its original Byzantine appearance despite Norman and later rebuilding. Gerace also remained one of the most strategic sites in southern Italy throughout the Middle Ages. The castle was finally destroyed by an earthquake in 1783.

the second half of the century they often formed over half of the available forces in supposedly feudal southern Italy.

Communal militias remained predominant to the north, but even here things were changing by the end of the century. Factionalism, rather than the resulting rule of oligarchies and aristocratic *signori*, was a major reason for the decline of the militias. Mercenaries, exiles from other towns or unemployed foreign troops, were also available, skilled and relatively cheap. Reliance on foreigners, supposedly untainted by local politics, had also proved its worth in the persons of those *podestas*— chief magistrates enlisted from outside—who had

already brought peace to a number of faction-torn Italian cities.

Given the riots, conspiracies and assassinations that characterised communal politics, it was hardly surprising that a ruling group felt disinclined to arm a city's population. At the same time reliable permanent forces were often needed, not to defend the walls but to garrison the extended frontiers of the *contado* or to attack a neighbouring commercial competitor. The *podestas'* guard often became the nucleus of a mercenary company. The 14th century also saw city-fathers increasingly handing over the defence of their state to a mercenary and his ready-made army, naming him Captain-General and drawing up the *condotta* or contract from which he and his followers got their name. Meanwhile the citizens settled down to earning the money to pay this condottiere and reserving their own abundant martial energies for ruthless political infighting.

## The Companies

While the year 1300 can be a convenient date to mark the mercenaries' emergence as the dominant element in Italian warfare, groups of troops with similar skills, such as French cavalry or Pisan crossbowmen, had long been recruited en bloc to form identifiable units. Not only was this easier for their paymaster, but the efficiency of such units was generally greater because its members knew their leader and had evolved both tactics and discipline.

Documentary records inevitably focus upon commanders, but the groups or Companies that these first condottieri led were still quite small. William della Torre, for example, rose from the mercenary ranks to appear on the Sienese payroll in 1285 at the head of 114 cavalry. One company of the first decade of the 14th century was some 300 strong, including both horse and foot, but this was an exception. So were those huge roving bands of plunderers who soon caught the eyes of contemporary chroniclers.

The seasonal and often short-term nature of Italian warfare made a mercenary's prospects very uncertain. All too often he was obliged to become an outlaw to feed himself. Many such men were foreigners and they soon found that their chances of success were greater if they operated in larger bands. Most of the largest companies of the early 14th century were, in fact, amalgamations of smaller units drawn together to survive a period of shortage. Perhaps for this reason they were very democratic. An overall leadership was elected, consultation among the troops preceded decisions, constables and counsellors shared the signing of contracts, and booty was divided according to rank and length of service.

Among these first 'free companies' were the Company of Siena operating in Umbria (1322–23), the Company of the Cerruglio operating around Lucca (1329–30) and the Cavalieri della Colomba operating in Lombardy and Tuscany (1334). German knights predominated in these associations, largely because of economic recession in Germany. Catalans also played a vital role, particularly among the leadership, which included William della Torre and Diego de Rat. The Catalan Grand Company which ravaged the Byzantine Empire around this time had its origins among Catalan troops brought to southern Italy by King Frederick of Aragon. Their leader was, however, an Italian of German extraction, Roger di Flor, who was called 'The Father of All Condottieri' by the Florentine historian Villani.

Italians were, in fact, already well to the fore although some also had territorial ambitions rather than simply a desire for employment.

The Rocca or Castle of Spoleto was built and completed by Matteo di Giovannello da Gubbio, called Gattaponi, between 1355 and 1361. It formed a linch-pin in the restoration of Papal authority in Umbria, undertaken by Cardinal Albornoz and his condottieri army. The regularity and simplicity of its plan, as well as its position on top of Monte S. Elia, make it a classic example of 14th century Italian fortification. (After Caciagli)

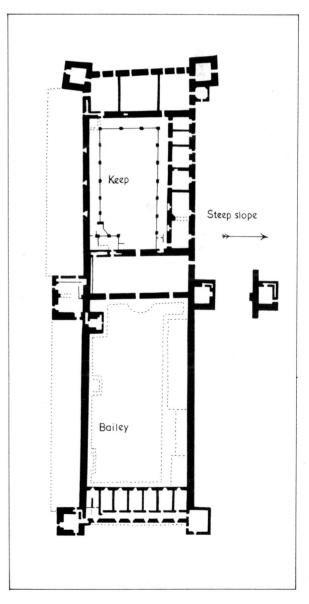

7

Castruccio Castracane, for example, served many princes before seizing power in his native Lucca, which he then ruled from 1314 to 1328. By contrast Guidoriccio da Fogliano was simply a soldier who faithfully served the Sienese (1327–34), in whose city his memory is preserved by Martini's splendid fresco, before being employed by Mastino della Scale of Verona.

The number of non-Italian mercenaries in early 14th century Italy was considerable—at least 10,000 German men-at-arms between 1320 and 1360 alone. Swiss and Catalans were already known, along with Provençals, Flemings, Castilians, French and English, while Hungarians appeared after 1347. The large companies they now formed were significant military forces. A leading

The statue of Cangrande della Scala, ruler of Verona, who died in 1329, originally stood with other statues on top of the Scaliger Tombs off the Piazza dei Signori; it is now preserved in the Castelvecchio Museum. The way Cangrande is carrying his great-helm on his back is almost certainly an inaccurate later restoration.

German condottiere, Werner von Ürslingen, was later credited with devising the 'plague of companies', but of course, he alone was not responsible. Nor was his the first of the much-feared 'free companies'. This honour should go to the Company of St. George formed by Lodrisio Visconti out of demobilised veterans from Verona in the vain hope of seizing control of his native Milan in 1339–40.

Werner von Ürslingen, one of its surviving leaders, then created the more effective Great Company two years later. Ürslingen and his successors alone gave continuity to the series of Great Companies seen throughout the 1340s and '50s. In 1342 one was recorded as including 3,000 cavalrymen plus an equal number of retainers. Some ten years later it consisted of 10,000 fighting men, including 7,000 cavalry and 2,000 crossbowmen, plus 20,000 camp-followers. Despite the unreliability of most medieval figures, such a total is not inconceivable. Its organisation was equally impressive, with an established commissariat and self-contained judicial system which included a portable gallows.

The Great Company, particularly under its later Provençal captain Montreal d'Albarno, was fully self-sufficient. It won booty by moving from city to city in search of protection-money, or by demanding redundancy pay before quitting another city's service. Some of these earnings were even invested in merchant ventures and money-lending. The ruthlessness of these early condottieri companies was never lived down by their more honourable successors; but their attitudes were quite typical of the 14th century, a time of turmoil, social change and the Black Death, which wiped out one third of the Italian population.

Yet, like its predecessors, even the Great Company had its failures. In 1342 a line of sharpened stakes backed by the determined militia infantry of Bologna denied Werner von Ürslingen's troops passage down the Val di Lamone for two months until an agreement was reached. In 1358, under Conrad von Landau, the Company was completely routed by Florentine militia crossbowmen and peasant levies, stiffened by a small contingent of mercenaries, again in a narrow valley. Attempting revenge the following

The rear of the massively fortified Palazzo Pubblico or Town Hall of Siena, built between 1288 and 1309. The top floor of the central section was added in the 16th century while the tower was erected between 1338 and 1348.

year, the Great Company was defeated even on ground of its own choosing. This time, however, the victors were a comparable mercenary force of Italians, Germans and Hungarians under Pandolfo Malatesta. Pandolfo was the first of this famous family to make a name as a condottiere. He was also one of a new breed, the Italian mercenary prince from the rugged Romagna region who offered himself and his military experience in exchange for the wealth denied him by his own poor patrimony. Another such man was Francesco degli Ordelaffi, whose family struggled long and hard to keep their lordship of Forlì out of Papal clutches.

## English Adventurers

When peace was reached between England and France in 1360, ending the first phase of the Hundred Years War, many English and other troops found themselves stranded. After ravaging the Rhône valley, about 6,000 accepted the leadership of Albert Sterz, a German, and went to fight for the Duke of Savoy against Milan.

In Italy they were called the White Company, and although the Italians referred to them as Inglesi this company included Germans, French, Scots and Welsh. Their name is said to have reflected the greater amount of plate armour they wore, which was also kept highly polished and uncovered. A generation or so later *armi bianchi*, or 'white armour', would describe the high quality steel armours worn without permanent coverings in which Milanese armourers excelled.

The dramatic success of the White Company

ANO·DNI·MCCCXXVIII

**The Condottiere leader Guidoriccio da Fogliano at the Sienese siege of Montemassi. This fresco in the Palazzo Pubblico, Siena, was painted by Simone Martini in 1328. (See MAA 50, *Medieval European Armies*, for colour reconstruction.)**

stemmed from its superior, but far from perfect, discipline, tactics evolved in the Hundred Years War, ferocity in battle and, not least, greater physical size. This latter feature also contributed to the number of Italian wives and daughters who were sent on prolonged holidays to cities not blessed by the protection of these foreign troops.

The White Company's cavalry, its men-at-arms, were divided into 'lances' of two soldiers—a *caporale* and his squire, though the former need not have been a dubbed knight—plus a *ragazzo* or page. Although they did fight on horseback, they also confounded their foes with infantry tactics in which the two men-at-arms held a single heavy lance as a pike. With their abundant plate armour they needed no shields, and could even act offensively by advancing in close ranks while pages brought up their horses in case of a sudden pursuit or retreat. Five 'lances' formed a 'post', five of which formed a *bandiera* or 'flag'.

An even more devastating innovation was the longbow. This completely outclassed the old simple short-bow, but lacked the range of the composite and crossbows. Yet it combined the rate of shooting of the former with the hitting power of the latter. Use of the longbow required strength and lengthy training, which English veterans of the French wars certainly had. Such longbowmen, though possessing horses, also invariably fought on foot. Longbows could be found in Italy, for example at Lucca. But rapid improvements in crossbows, the increasing adoption of hand-held firearms and the influence of newer, post-Mongol forms of oriental-style composite bows on such trading states as Venice and Genoa, made the White Company's longbows a short-lived if dramatic phenomenon in Italian warfare.

The White Company was also noted for its portable siege equipment, its light artillery, and its willingness to fight at night, all of which gave these mercenaries exceptional strategic flexibility.

# The Great Captains

Sir John Hawkwood was elected leader of the White Company in 1364, and from then on this Company's character gradually changed. Increasingly it became Sir John's army rather than one of those free-ranging, self-sufficient forces seen earlier.

Hawkwood, described by Froissart as 'a poor knight having earned nothing but his spurs', came from Sible Hedingham in Essex and, after winning his knighthood on the field of Poitiers in 1345, served Edward III faithfully until the advent of peace. He followed his erstwhile comrades to Italy late in 1363 and, after the White Company broke up outside Florence the following year, Albert Sterz led a section renamed the Company of the Star southward while Hawkwood took over the remainder.

Building on the established reputation of the Inglesi and by imposing even firmer discipline, Sir John moulded the White Company into a personal army which, with his record of generalship and loyalty, won very lucrative contracts. Neither he nor his soldiers were paragons of virtue, however. At Faenza in 1376, and to an even worse degree at Cesena the following year, they joined other Papal mercenaries in massacring the civilian population as part of Cardinal Robert of Geneva's reprisal campaign. Condottieri armies were also noted for the presence of numerous prostitutes in their baggage-train and, judging by their reputations in Pisa and Florence, the White Company was no exception.

Roving mercenary armies did not suddenly disappear, of course, and the four major companies operating in Italy around 1365 still had their own names. They were, however, generally better known by those of their commanders—Hawkwood, Sterz, Hannekin Bongarten and Ambrogio Visconti. Most also split up on the death or retirement of their captain. These latter were increasingly drawn into the ranks of the local feudal aristocracy, even including Hawkwood, who received the towns of Cotignola and Bagnacavallo from the Pope.

One of the last foreign companies consisted of Bretons led by Bertrand de la Salle. A second Company of the Star emerged in 1379, while the last of them all, the small Company of the Rose, survived until 1410. Major reasons for the companies' decline included a series of Leagues, or city alliances, aimed specifically against them; the growing power and decreasing numbers of independent Italian states; and the increasing

The early 14th century fortified tower-houses on the north side of the Piazza del Duomo in San Gimignano acted as individual family castles in this strife-torn town. Such towers were once characteristic of many medieval Italian cities.

pay offered to men who accepted long-term service with one such state.

It was popularly assumed, in Italy and elsewhere, that foreign mercenaries dominated Italian battlefields in the 14th century. In fact, this is a gross oversimplification. On the other hand, the importance of foreigners did decline at the end of that century. Few Italian states could afford to hire the major companies, and inter-communal war invariably began with each city relying on its own militia, plus a few mercenaries. Nevertheless, the availability of condottieri normally meant that the richer side won the war.

Italian commanders were also among the most successful. Ambroglio Visconti, a bastard son of that amazing Milanese family, was a comrade and rival of the foreigner Hawkwood. He established the Company of San Giorgio in 1365, a name that was to feature prominently in the Italian military

Infantrymen fighting with sword and buckler on frescoes in the castle of Sabbionara at Avio, in the Trento. Painted around 1340, these illustrate the almost perpetual state of conflict between the Ghibeline, or pro-Holy Roman Empire, family of Castelbarco who held Sabbionara and the Guelph, or pro-Papacy, forces of the neighbouring Bishop of Trento. They provide some of the best pictures of 14th century north Italian infantry.

revival towards the end of the century. Then, however, it was a third Company of San Giorgio, predominantly Italian like its predecessors, which followed a man who made a point of emphasising traditional Italian tactics. He was Alberico da Barbiano and although his first great victory was over foreigners—Bretons—Alberico's Company of San Giorgio just as often fought alongside Englishmen, Germans and Hungarians. Another successful Italian captain was Facino Cane.

Yet it was Barbiano who became the folk-hero of Italy's military renaissance. His conscious Italianism even extended to tactics and the consequent equipment of his troops. Condottieri warfare had always been characterised by dramatic strategy, large-scale manoeuvre, an avoidance of unnecessary battles, and an abundance of inconclusive sieges. Barbiano believed that Hawkwood's preference for dismounting his men-at-arms undermined the status of the knightly class. This prejudice was, however, based on sound military considerations, for a small corps of highly trained cavalry impressed a potential employer far more than did a comparable investment in infantry. Militias could still provide sufficient of these. Italian cavalry armour also now increased in weight, following fashions in France and England, while infantry armour almost disappeared. Barbiano and others favoured the visored bascinet—which tended to replace both the old great helm and even the newer sallet among heavy cavalry—as well as the use of more extensive horse-armour. Such equipment for horse and rider was primarily a defence against infantry weapons like bows and pikes.

Florence, that bastion of republicanism, retained a preference for foreign condottieri, with the Gascon Bernardon de Serres succeeding Hawkwood. Milan, under the skilful rule of Gian Galeazzo Visconti, meanwhile recruited as many star condottieri as possible. Bernabo Visconti had started this trend by marrying five of his illegitimate daughters to leading mercenaries. Gian Galeazzo continued by keeping Jacopo dal Verme in his service for 30 years, and enlisting Alberigo da Barbiano, Facino Cane, Ugolotto Biancardo, Ottobuono Terzo and both Pandolfo and Carlo Malatesta, thus mopping up almost all the leading talent.

These men and their followers not only dominated most Italian battlefields. They were also capable of defeating the best that Italy's neighbours could produce. In 1368 the condottieri system halted the Emperor Charles IV of Germany at Borgoforte, although both armies were equally mixed. Venetian mercenaries were fighting successfully against Turks and practically everyone else in the eastern Mediterranean, while back in northern Italy Milanese forces defeated the French at Alessandria in 1391 and the Germans at Brescia in 1401.

Efficient as it was, condottieri warfare was also very expensive. As early as 1362 Florence established a system of interest-free loans drawn from public funds to support financially embarrassed warriors. Two years later that same city paid 100,000 gold florins to bribe an enemy mercenary army, while it has been estimated that 14th century Popes sometimes spent 60 per cent of their revenues on warfare. Other states are unlikely to have differed. The result was greatly increased taxation, bureaucracy, banking and credit facilities and further centralisation of political power. The condottiere's greatest impact in Italy was less on the art of war than on the art of government!

## Sforzeschi and Bracceschi

Men with political ambitions were found among the condottieri from the start, but they certainly became more common by the end of the 14th century. Confusion in the Papal States and Naples had always offered them scope, and many were exiled petty nobility from this area who hoped to return as masters of their native cities. When Gian Galeazzo Visconti died in 1402, however, the subsequent near-anarchy in northern Italy was greatly to the advantage of the political soldier.

The Duchy of Milan lost many of its newly acquired territories and went through a period of confusion. Three condottieri, Pandolfo Malatesta, Terzo and Fondulo, withdrew from Milanese service and won control of Brescia, Parma and Cremona respectively. Dal Verme stayed faithful to the Visconti while Carlo Malatesta already had his ancestral powerbase in Rimini. Facino Cane also remained in Milanese employ, but at the same time established himself in Alessandria while

Few towns in northern Italy preserve complete medieval city walls in a visible state, but those of Montagnana, near Padua, are fine examples of urban defences from the pre-gunpowder era. They probably survived because Montagnana was of minor strategic importance and remained firmly under Venetian control after Venice conquered the lordship of Padua early in the 15th century.

working towards domination of Milan itself. Eventually Facino did win control, but failed to destroy the Visconti dynasty.

Hardly surprisingly, Florentine suspicion of the condottieri deepened. Its preference for the militia was also reinforced by the rising tide of Renaissance civic humanist ideology—an ideology which, at least in the military field, was soon to fail. By contrast, Venetian expansion across northern Italy opened up a lucrative new field at the start of the 15th century. Subsequent wars between Venice and Hungary merely reinforced this trend.

Both the Malatesta brothers now served Venice, but they are also interesting as representatives of the new breed of cultured condottieri. Carlo and Pandolfo were, in fact, true Renaissance princes with their Latin humanist educations and patronage of the arts.

There was less time for the arts in southern Italy, but continuing scope for the ambitious soldier. The Kingdom of Naples was again torn between Angevin and Aragonese dynastic claims, while Rome was simultaneously struggling to reassert its control over the Papal States following a crushing Neapolitan invasion. Both Pope and Neapolitan king now commanded large military forces consisting of similarly inflated condottieri companies. It was here that the two men whose

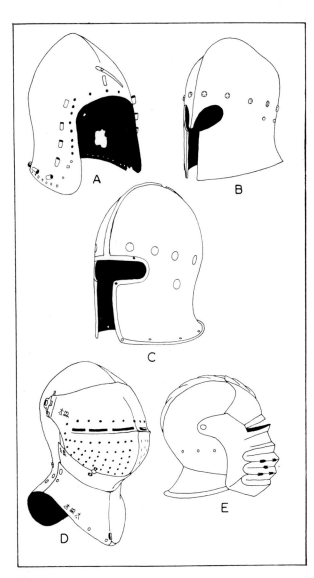

Some Italian helmets from the time of the condottieri A Barbuta with attachment for a visor, mid-15th century (Museum für Deutsche Geschichte, Berlin). B Barbuta-sallet, probably inspired by an ancient Greek 'Corinthian' helmet and probably made in the Missaglia workshops, Milan, 1430–1445 (Wallace Coll., London). C Venetian sallet, possibly made in Milan around 1455 (Wallace Coll., London). D Great bascinet, part of a complete armour made in Milan by Tomaso Negroni da Ello, called Missaglia, probably in 1450, for the Elector Palatine Frederick I (Waffensammlung, Vienna). E Visored sallet, probably Milanese, from around 1500 (Armoury of the Knights of St. John, Valetta)

of his native town of Cotignola in 1411. Braccio da Montone, though nobly born, worked his way up the condottiere ladder more slowly. Like Sforza he had been a follower and pupil of Barbiano, but this Perugian soldier also had a reputation, not only for courage, but also for impetuosity. Frequently captured and almost as often wounded, Braccio was nevertheless generally successful.

It was Sforza who really inherited Barbiano's tactical concepts. He both inspired loyalty and emphasised discipline, and this enabled him to control his troops to an exceptional degree. This in turn permitted more than the usual amount of forward planning. On the other hand Sforza was a very cautious general who relied on massed units and, unlike his teacher, large numbers of infantry. Braccio was far from being cautious, though he similarly inspired loyalty and thus controlled his troops. By emphasising cavalry and dividing them into distinct squadrons, he could commit his men to battle in short bursts, 'rotating' units to bring fresh troops up at intervals.

These men inspired two schools of tactical thought which long outlived their founders. Though their differences were clearer in theory than on the battlefield, the Sforzeschi and Bracceschi became 'teams' behind which Italian factionalism could rally, much as it had behind the labels Guelph and Ghibelline in a previous century.

# State Armies

Real changes were seen in military organisation and recruitment during the early 15th century. Prolonged warfare had already inflated the armies of Naples and the Papal States. Thirty years of conflict, from 1424 onwards, would similarly alter the armies of Milan, Florence and Venice. The days of the Great Captains were passing, as had those of the Free Companies. Condottieri still led the way but behind them marched state-administered, almost national, armies.

The Palazzo Vecchio in Florence, begun in 1298 but constantly added to in the following centuries, is perhaps the best-known Italian fortified civic building from the time of the Communes.

names dominated Italian tactics won their reputations.

Musio Attendolo, better known as Sforza, came from a wealthy but non-noble family in the Romagna. He was destined for a military career from childhood and was soon serving Alberigo da Barbiano as a squadron commander. His rise was rapid, and he was rewarded by being made count

Unlike Germany, where civilian entrepreneurs were increasingly responsible for mustering troops, Italian condottieri remained soldiers and did their own recruiting. Mercenaries were, however, demanding longer contracts and greater security of employment. This is clearly reflected in surviving contracts. A *condotta* would normally specify the numbers, types, units and equipment of soldiers. Next it would lay down the agreement's duration, which was normally in two parts—a *ferma* or set period of service and *di rispetto*, an optional extension which often led to almost continuous service. Next came the rate of pay, normally including an advance. During the 15th century longer-term contracts, in which a retainer was paid even during periods of peace, became increasingly common.

To supervise the soldiers and ensure adherence to the *condotta*, an employer would appoint *provveditori*, or civilian commissioners, to accompany the army. Needless to say, such *provveditori* were rarely popular with the condottieri. Employers naturally wanted quick, cheap victories while soldiers preferred safe and, if possible, long-term employment. Nevertheless, most cities showed a marked preference for cautious, calculating and above all safe military leaders. Fidelity, organisation and security apparently impressed them more than did bravery or even outstanding success.

It is widely believed that the military reforms of Charles VII of France in 1439 created western Europe's first standing army since ancient times. Yet French chroniclers like Philippe de Commynes clearly stated that Charles imitated various Italian princes. Italian armies were, in fact, becoming more permanent throughout the 15th century. In addition to, and gradually replacing, the hurriedly recruited mercenary companies were units whose terms of service were virtually open-ended.

Garrison units were naturally the first such permanent troops and were known as *provisionati*, from their regular wage or *provisione*. While most *provisionati* were infantry, some were cavalry. Generally, however, the new permanently employed horseman was known as a *lanze spezzate*. This meant 'broken lance' and stemmed from the fact that many of the first had either deserted from condottieri companies or came from those whose leaders had died. By the 1430s *provisionati* and *lanzi spezzati* were common in most Italian armies. Late in the century Milan and Venice also evolved a new structure of properly trained and paid militia, many of them hand-gunners, who were available for full-time service in case of emergency. They were similarly called *provisionati*.

Italian armies were growing very large. Some Milanese and Venetian field forces reached 20,000 men between 1425 and 1454, despite the fact that these states often had to fight on two fronts. Other 15th century Italian armies generally ranged between 4,000 and 18,000 men. In addition most could also field large numbers of auxiliary infantry.

Standing armies and large field forces inevitably meant a permanent administrative structure; and professional paymasters, provisioners, quartermasters and transport officers were soon in great demand to support the traditional *provedditori*. Most important of them all were the *collaterali* who oversaw these new administrative structures. Interestingly enough, most states now preferred a local, or at least newly resident, military leadership. Where possible outsiders were encouraged to settle, being given palaces or citizenship if their performances merited it. Venetian commanders tended to come from the nobility of Terraferma towns like Bergamo and Brescia, rather than from the island-city of Venice itself. In the Papal States military leadership often now went either to Roman nobility like the ancient Orsini family, or, via a system of blatant nepotism, to the current Pope's own clan. In Naples this preference went so far as to forbid Neapolitan barons from serving other Italian states. Meanwhile Florence again remained aloof from such trends, and paid for it with less than satisfactory armies.

**Cavalry and Infantry in a Renaissance Army**
Italian Renaissance warfare with its continuing reliance on heavy cavalry was not, as has so often been suggested, out of date. The role of heavily armoured cavalry, which has itself been exaggerated, had sound military justification, even though it did set 15th century Italian armies somewhat apart from their European neighbours. Most Italian heavy cavalry were still condottieri

recruited in the traditional way. They predominated numerically in the mid-15th century but had declined to a minority in most armies by 50 years later. Naturally, the proportion of one sort of troops to another depended on the nature of the forthcoming campaign. Even a condottieri company, despite its core of heavily armoured horsemen, increasingly included light cavalry and infantry. The size of the basic unit, the lance, was also growing. A four-man lance appeared in Milan in the 1470s, and five-man *corazzas* in the Papal States a decade earlier. Progressively heavier armour for the man-at-arms and his mount meant that horses tired more quickly. So more horses, and thus more attendants, were consequently needed. It is, however, far from clear whether the enlarged cavalry unit had more or differently equipped fighting men, or simply more pages. Broader units were also being standardised. The old rough guide, that a squadron consisted of 25 lances, became a reality while the condottieri band, or *condotte*, was similarly normally fixed at 50 or 100 lances.

Light cavalry, as opposed to support horsemen such as the pages, were needed because of the more sophisticated nature of 15th century warfare. Tasks like scouting, foraging and pursuit were sometimes carried out by men whose primary rôle was that of mounted infantry crossbowmen and hand-gunners. But the most effective and dramatic light cavalry were newcomers to the Italian scene. These *stradiotti* were mostly of Albanian or Greek origin and had long been recruited by Venice for her overseas wars. They first appeared in Italy around 1470 and their normal weapons consisted of light lances, javelins and sometimes bows or crossbows. The military heritage of such *stradiotti* was Byzantine, though with a new Turkish element added. After the short Ottoman occupation of Otranto in 1480, Naples enlisted 1,500 Turkish cavalry who then fought in northern Italy against Venice and her *stradiotti*.

The primary rôle of Italian infantry had long been in sieges, though with a subsidiary defensive function in open battle. Now, however, an increasing use of field fortifications gave added importance to the foot soldier. Field fortifications, such as trench-works, were in fact the single most significant development in 15th century Italian

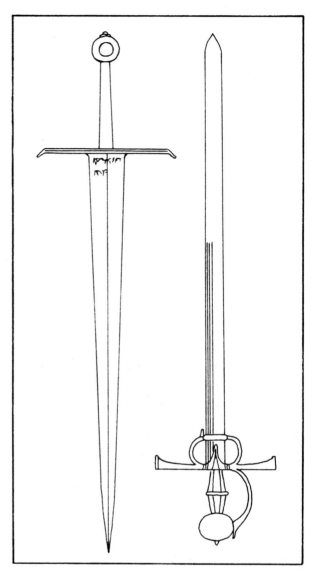

LEFT **Italian 'sword of war' of the mid-14th century, probably captured by the Egyptian Mamlūks from a Cypriot force that unsuccessfully besieged Alexandria in 1365 (Metropolitan Museum of Art, New York).** RIGHT **Venetian sword decorated with imitation Islamic ornament, late 15th century (Metropolitan Museum of Art, New York)**

warfare. Since the decline of the old urban militias, Italy lacked an infantry tradition comparable to those of the English archer or the Swiss pikeman. But in response to warfare in the broad, flat Lombard plain with its patchwork of rivers and canals, a new type of infantry appeared. This was the Italian sword-and-buckler foot soldier. Lightly equipped and trained for offensive fighting, he mirrored, though was not necessarily inspired by, certain types of Spanish infantry who had, in

'Arrest of St. James', detail of a panel made by Leonardo di Ser Giovanni in 1371, on the right side of the Pistoia Cathedral silver altar. Note the large shield, similar to examples found in some earlier frescoes.

turn, been modelled on the Muslim mountaineers of Granada. Crossbowmen remained vital but were increasingly supplanted by hand-gunners, who were easier to train and whose weapons were cheaper to produce.

The earliest Italian hand-gun, the *schiopetto*, may even have been known in the late 13th century. *Schiopettieri*, hand-gunners, were certainly increasingly numerous among the fixed garrisons of the 14th and early 15th centuries. By then similarly armed units were also included in many field armies. The large numbers of Milanese hand-gunners clearly worried the Venetians in the 1440s; and their importance was firmly established by 1482 when, during the War of Ferrara, the Milanese had 1,250 hand-guns and only 233 crossbows. This force also included 352 arque-buses, a far more effective firearm with a spring-

'Trial and Condemnation of St. James', detail of another panel by Ser Giovanni on the Pistoia silver altar. Here a knight in heavier armour, including a laminated fauld to protect his abdomen, is the central figure.

loaded trigger which brought the burning match to the flash-pan. By 1490 even some mounted infantry were being armed with the arquebus in the Papal States.

The role of cannon was less dramatic in the 15th century. They were still used mostly in siege warfare and, because of their size, cumbersome carriages and very slow rates of fire, proved far more efficient in defence than in attack. In open battle field artillery were most effective in ambush, where again they could be carefully positioned. Nevertheless, field fortifications did provide increasing scope for the use of cannon. In fact, 15th century artillery raised the cost of war rather than having any profound impact on the art of warfare.

The 15th century also saw an outpouring of military treatises comparable only to Rome as it

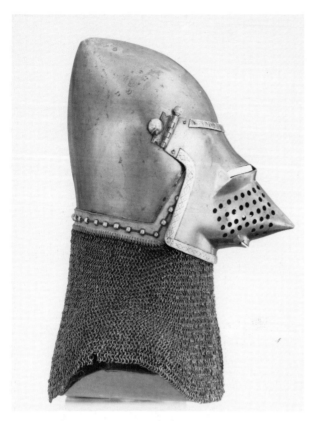

tottered to its fall, Islam as it was menaced by the Mongols, and Europe in the declining years of the failed Crusading ideal. These were all times of crisis, but how much the political turbulence of Renaissance Italy contributed to such military theorising is unclear. It may simply have been just another aspect of that Renaissance infatuation with the Classical past from which the theorists drew most of their morals. It does seem highly unlikely that the later condottieri imitated Roman tactics, though they may well have been flattered by any parallels between themselves and Caesar.

# 'Good War'-'Bad War'

The increasing savagery of warfare in later 15th century Italy led to widespread concern about the differences between 'good' and 'bad' war. Devastation, the attempt to undermine an opponent's economy by the destruction of crops, mills, and so on, had long been normal practice. Here, however, peasants rather than soldiers suffered most. The actual *quastatori*, or devastators, were normally peasants conscripted as pioneers, which also enabled the warrior class to remain at least slightly aloof.

Machiavelli's propagandist myth of bloodless condottieri battles should long since have been put to rest. Casualties had always been higher in siege-warfare, however, particularly when a direct assault proved necessary. In open battle the issue was rarely fought out to the bitter end. During the 15th century the use of gunpowder certainly led to higher losses, not least because bullet wounds were dirtier and involved the destruction of more tissue, so tending to fester more often. Foreign troops such as *stradiotti*, who were paid a ducat for every enemy head, and Frenchmen and Spaniards, who often dispatched their fallen foes with daggers, also made warfare more hazardous.

On the other hand, Italian armies had surprisingly good medical services. Neapolitan army doctors ranked equal to the feudal nobility and helped both officers and common soldiers. Records show some of their operations in the field to have been astonishing, if somewhat chancy. The treat-

A Milanese bascinet with a hounskull visor, plus the original mail aventail. (Formerly in Churburg, Alto Adige, now in the Tower of London Armoury, inv. IV 430)

nent of prisoners in condottieri warfare seems to
have been far more humane than elsewhere in
Europe, where only the wealthy could normally be
expected to be taken for ransom. In Italy the
ordinary soldier was generally merely stripped of
his weapons and set free. States had no facilities
for large numbers of PoWs, while slavery was
reserved for captured Muslims, not for fellow
Christians. Mutilation of captured troops to
ensure that they never fought again was regarded
as the epitome of 'bad war'.

In contrast to such attitudes, the Italian
commander was prepared to use poison to remove
the enemy's leadership, to encourage treachery,
deceipt and desertion, to employ ruthless scorched-
earth policies, and to terrorise the foe by the
bestial treatment of enemy corpses.

*   *   *

Italy fell under foreign domination early in the
16th century and it was widely assumed, then
and now, that this was at least partly because of
the failure of Italian arms. Thus, by extension, the
condottieri have been blamed.

Yet Italian commanders were far from ignorant
of warfare beyond the Alps. Discounting Venetian
and Genoese involvement in the Middle East,
Italian warriors served in many parts of the world.
Pippo Spano, a Florentine condottiere, spent most
of his highly successful career in Hungary.
Genoese crossbowmen served in France, as did a
Milanese expeditionary force in 1465. Southern
Italians fought as exiles in France, Burgundy and
Spain. Burgundy remained, in fact, a favoured
employer among Italian mercenaries during the
second half of this century. Others went to
Germany.

Throughout the 15th century Italian armies
had defeated most, though not all, incursions by
hostile neighbours, be they French, Swiss, German,
Austrian, Hungarian or Turkish. At Calliano in
1487 the Venetians met, and more than held their
own against, German *landsknechte* and Swiss
infantry, troops who were then regarded as the
best in Europe.

Yet there is little doubt that the French
invasion of 1494 heralded an era of military
decline, if not disaster, for Italy. The Italian

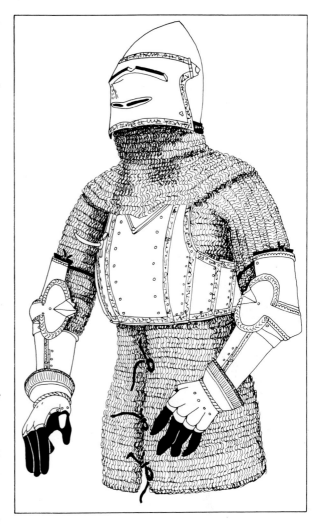

A composite Milanese armour from the armoury of the
Vogt family, bailiffs of Matsch. It was probably made in the
Missaglia workshops around 1380–1390. The leg defences are
missing (Churburg Castle, no. 13, Alto Adige)

failure was political rather than military, and
stemmed from disunity and a lack of political
determination. With the involvement of 16th
century Europe's two super-powers, France and
Spain, Italy became an international battlefield
on which Italians fought for both sides. Nevertheless, it is worth noting that French armies relied on
large cavalry forces and massed infantry pikemen
while striving for a crushing victory in a set-piece
battle. By contrast the Spaniards had a numerical
strength comparable to that of the French, but
adopted the smaller armies, the emphasis on
manoeuvre, broad strategy and siege-warfare
that had been evolved by Italian condottieri.
Spain also emerged as the victor.

Sienese forces at the battle of Sinalunga, 1363, in which Siena defeated the freebooting condottieri Compagnia del Capello led by Niccolò da Montefeltro. This fresco by Lippo Vanni is in the Palazzo Pubblico, Siena. Note crossbow emblem on flags.

# Campaigns

## Lucca (1329–30)

The Republic of Lucca had long been a rival of Pisa, which in turn was a deadly rival of Genoa. Thus Lucca was squeezed between two larger and mutually antipathetic neighbours. Despite its lack of a major port, Lucca had dominated much of western Tuscany under the leadership of Castruccio Castracani, a one-time condottiere. After his death in 1328 Lucca remained prosperous and had clearly already extended beyond its new walls, enclosing suburbs which themselves had spread beyond the original Roman defences. These new fortifications of 1260 included a deep ditch. In 1329 a large army under the Holy Roman Emperor, Louis of Bavaria, was based at the neighbouring city of Pisa. Some 800 German mercenary cavalry, perhaps behind with their

pay, deserted the Imperial camp and made an unauthorised attack on Lucca. They probably marched along the old road around Monte Pisano, although such a mounted force might have attempted to bypass the Luccan frontier castle of Nozzano by going directly over Monte Pisano, a route followed by the modern main road. How much surprise the Germans achieved is unclear, for they were unable to seize a gate and, lacking siege equipment, could not attempt the walls. Nevertheless the eastern suburbs provided plenty of loot. The raiding force then retired to neighbouring hills, probably Monte Serra to the south, where, at an unidentified spot, they established a winter camp called the Cerruglio. The Emperor Louis sent a nobleman named Marco Visconti to negotiate with the German mercenaries but, in the event, they elected him as their leader and named themselves the Company of the Cerruglio. The following spring this condottieri company again swooped on Lucca and this time seized the city in a coup de main. More loot was acquired, to which the Company added 30,000 gold florins by selling the city to its increasingly powerful neighbour, Genoa. The Company of the Cerruglio

had probably been formed solely to plunder Lucca; once the rewards had been shared, the association ended and its members dispersed.

**Heavy cavalry in action at the battle of Sinalunga. The heraldic devices of the victorious Sienese, on the left, almost certainly represent those of actual participants.**

## Parabiago (1340)

In contrast to the skilfully executed plunder of Lucca, the battle of Parabiago seems to have involved little in the way of tactics save for the impromptu commitment of reserves. Perhaps for this reason, Parabiago saw exceptionally heavy casualties. The Company of St. George, the first condottieri association to bear that name, was, like various previous companies, formed for a specific campaign. In 1339 many mercenaries, demobilised following the Della Scala wars in Verona, took service under Lodrisio Visconti. This exiled member of the family that had dominated Milan since 1277 intended to oust his Visconti cousins, Azzo and Lucchino, from the leadership of the city. To this end he hired 2,500 cavalry, mostly German, and 1,000 infantry, many of them Swiss, under the co-leadership of two German mercenaries, Werner of Ürslingen and Conrad of Landau. As the Company of St. George marched westward, north of Milan

towards Legnano, Lucchino Visconti summoned the Milanese militia and recruited his own condottieri, including an Italian force of 700 cavalry led by Ettore da Panigo from Bologna. Events moved quickly and in February 1340, with snow thick on the ground and the irrigation canals probably frozen, the Company of St. George made a sudden attack on the Milanese advance guard at Parabiago. These troops, probably mostly militia, were encamped near the present Villoresi Canal. The Germans and Swiss, more accustomed to the weather, broke the advance guard and pursued it towards Milan until they met the main Milanese army. Although substantially outnumbering the Company of St. George, the Milanese were almost overwhelmed in a vigorous assault, Lucchino Visconti being captured and tied to a tree. It says much for the communal spirit of the militia that, unlike most medieval armies, it did not collapse with the loss of its leader. Instead a confused resistance was maintained until Ettore da Panigo's cavalry hurriedly came up from Milan. The

Company of St. George was in turn routed. Lodrisio Visconti was captured and Lucchino released, while over 4,000 dead from both sides remained on the field.

## Castagnaro (1387)

Many of the most famous condottieri of the late 14th century took part in the battle of Castagnaro, which also provides an interesting example of defensive tactics inspired by English successes in the Hundred Years War. The opposing forces consisted of the Veronese, led by Giovanni dei Ordelaffi from Forli, and the Paduans under the English condottiere Sir John Hawkwood. Hawkwood's army of 7,000 mounted men-at-arms, 1,000 infantry and 600 English archers equipped as mounted infantry, had been besieging Verona for some weeks. But this force proved too small and its lines of communication were in danger of being cut, so, early in March, Hawkwood retreated some 50 kilometres down the west bank of the River Adige towards his supply depot at Castelbaldo. The Veronese followed closely and increased their strength by collecting outlying raiding forces. Ordelaffi expected the Paduans to cross the river into Castelbaldo, but instead Hawkwood instructed the base-commander to ferry waggon-

**The Battle of Castagnaro, 1387.**

loads of provisions across the Adige to meet hi retreating force at Castagnaro. This would sugges that Hawkwood already intended to make a stand west of the river. He even seems to have surprised his own subordinates by not merely making camp at Castagnaro on the night of 10 March, but by arranging his troops in a strong defensive array The strength of their position was as much a result of recent weather as of terrain. Along the Paduans' front ran an irrigation drain, probably the winding Scola Castagnare, part of which is still called the Old Drain. To the Paduans' right lay a large canal linking the Adige and the Tartaro rivers. Both drain and canal join the Adige at the same point. Here various dykes overlook an expanse of shallow shoals that lie uncovered except during floods. A stretch of marsh, now drained, protected the Paduans' left flank. To the north-west the meadows were also damp and soft after recent rain.

Hawkwood was up early, arranging his men in two dismounted lines. A third mounted rank stood slightly to the rear, with the Paduan *carroccio* and Hawkwood's own troop of mounted English archers. His infantry crossbowmen were placed on the extreme right where, supported by the Paduans' few bombards, they covered those shallows where drain, canal and river met.

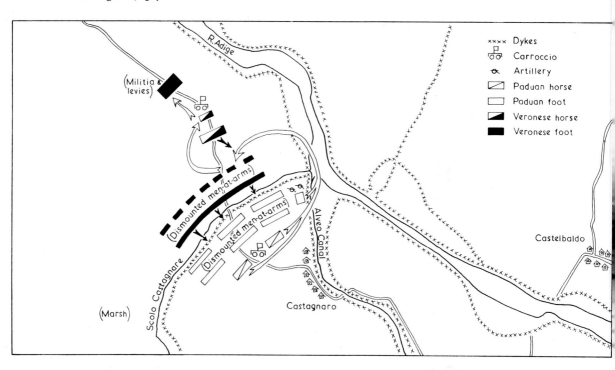

| | |
|---|---|
| xxxx | Dykes |
| | Carroccio |
| | Artillery |
| | Paduan horse |
| | Paduan foot |
| | Veronese horse |
| | Veronese foot |

A

1: North Italian infantryman, mid-14th C.
2: North Italian crossbowman, mid-14th C.
3: Venetian infantryman, first half 14th C.

B

1: Italian army commander, mid-14th C.
2: Austrian man-at-arms, mid-14th C.
3: English bowman, mid-14th C.

C

1: Lombard knight, late 14th C.
2: North Italian handgunner, late 14th C.
3: Italian heavy infantryman, late 14th C.

1: Italian knight, c.1425
2: Italian light infantryman, first half 15th C.
3: Artilleryman, early 15th C.

E

1: North Italian light cavalryman, c.1460
2: Italian knight, c.1460

F

1: Siennese crossbowman, late 15th C.
2: Venetian colonial archer, late 15th C.
3: Venetian heavy infantryman, late 15th C.

G

1: Spanish man-at-arms, end of 15th C.
2: Italian knight, end of 15th C.
3: French handgunner, end of 15th C.

Ordelaffi now had a force of 9,000 mounted men-at-arms, 2,600 infantry crossbowmen and pikemen, plus a large number of barely trained militia with whom he had expected to besiege Castelbaldo. The Veronese commander's artillery, 24 bombards and three experimental multi-barrelled ribaulds, were trailing some way to the rear and do not seem to have reached the battle. Ordelaffi spent most of the morning of the 11th arranging the bulk of his troops for an infantry assault on the Paduan position. The soft ground and assorted water obstacles seemingly ruled out a cavalry attack. They also prepared numerous fascines, or bundles of reeds, to fill the ditch. The dismounted Veronese men-at-arms stood in two lines supported by a small cavalry reserve. To their rear was the *carroccio* of Verona defended by 300 horsemen, while the militia and peasant levies stood even further back.

Ordelaffi ordered an assault shortly after noon, but his first line failed to cross the ditch. The Veronese second line was then sent forward in a selective manner while the fascines steadily filled several sections of ditch. A determined pushing match between spearmen now developed along parts of the dyke. Hawkwood sent his second line to support the first, while Ordelaffi committed all his second line, plus some of the militia. The outnumbered Paduans had to give ground so that the ditch no longer provided a defence. On the other hand the Veronese no longer had effective reserves, so Hawkwood delivered his masterstroke. Unlike Ordelaffi, he knew that it was possible for a mounted force to get around the north-eastern edge of the battle, probably along the stony river shallows and perhaps even hidden by dykes. Suddenly Hawkwood led his mounted English archers, plus the mounted men-at-arms, around his right flank, collecting the Paduan crossbowmen and gunners as he went. On reaching the Veronese rear, the archers and crossbowmen released a volley before they and the cavalry hit the enemy's left flank. This halted the Veronese advance and was immediately followed by a counter-attack led by the Paduan second-in-command, Ubaldini. Hawkwood threw his commander's baton into the midst of the enemy as an encouragement for his men to retrieve it, presumably in expectation of a reward, while

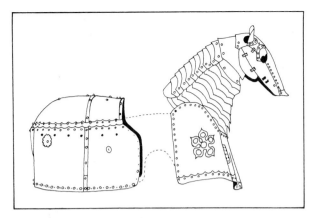

The earliest surviving example of a medieval European bard, or horse-armour. It was made by Pier Innocenzo da Faerno's workshop in Milan around 1450. (City of Vienna Historical Museum)

Ordelaffi charged with his own cavalry reserve in an attempt to relieve the situation. They were, however, hindered by their own retreating comrades, and after a brief struggle surrendered. Hawkwood had wheeled about to lead his horsemen against the Veronese *carroccio*, which was captured without much resistance. The militia and peasant levies largely fled, except for an infantry detachment under Giovanni da Isola which, for some reason, refused to surrender and was wiped out. The Paduans captured all the leading condottieri who were fighting for Verona, plus 4,600 men-at-arms and 800 infantry. Total casualties were listed as 716 dead and 846 wounded; only about 100 dead came from the Paduan side, while Veronese losses were greatly inflated by the unexplained defiance of Da Isola's detachment.

## Alessandria (1391)

One of the most successful Italian condottieri of the late 14th century was Jacopo dal Verme, two of whose relatives had fought on the losing side at Castagnaro. Jacopo similarly faced Hawkwood, though often with greater success. Jacopo dal Verme had long been Captain-General to Gian Galeazzo Visconti of Milan, the most powerful ruler in northern Italy. Powerful, rich and economically highly developed as the Duchy of Milan was, it also remained a small state with some large kingdoms uncomfortably close to its borders. The most threatening of these was France which, by the end of the 14th century, had not only won the first part of its Hundred Years

War against England but was now casting covetous eyes on Milan. The French controlled the small County of Asti through a dynastic marriage which also gave France some claim to the Milanese Dukedom. Now there was also French occupation of Naples, a French alliance with Milan's perpetual enemy Florence, and a pro-French Pope. When French garrisons were invited into the Republic of Genoa and a series of Florentine victories neutralized previously pro-Milanese states in northern Italy, Milan's position was clearly threatened. Dal Verme also knew that a strategic plan had been prepared whereby Hawkwood's Florentines would attack from the east while the French under the Count of Armagnac advanced from the west. In Milan's favour were her unity of command, interior lines of communication across flat countryside supplied with generally good roads, plus an excellent intelligence system. Invaders would almost inevitably have to approach either across mountains or a series of rivers.

The 14th century Porta S. Agostino formed the lower gate of the tiny fortified town of Montefalco, near Perugia. Sometimes called the Balcony of Umbria because of its altitude of nearly 500m., Montefalco was of vital strategic importance, first to the Lombard Duchy of Spoleto and later to the Papal States.

In mid-May Hawkwood opened the campaign by crossing the Adige, then the Mincio and other rivers flowing south from the Swiss Alps. But Dal Verme made no move for, like Hawkwood, he expected a French army to appear from the west. The Florentines came within 50 kilometres of Milan until, with supply lines stretched and still no word of the French, Hawkwood felt he had won a moral victory and so began a steady withdrawal. Dal Verme now followed in a cautious pursuit while sending the Florentines courteous challenges to combat. The Milanese had reached Lodi and Hawkwood no longer posed a threat when news of the Count of Armagnac arrived. The French were descending on the strategically vital but well fortified Milanese frontier citadel of Alessandria. This faced the small, hilly County of Asti, now a major French base, and the mountain passes south towards Genoa, while behind its protection lay the broad plains of Lombardy. A series of forced marches from Lodi enabled Dal Verme's troops to catch the French completely by surprise beneath the walls of Alessandria. This time there were none of the courtesies previously seen between the two fellow-professionals, Dal Verme and Hawkwood. Instead, on 25 July, the Italians virtually annihilated the French army, slaying the Count of Armagnac and most of his leading knights. The surviving invaders fled back to the mountain passes, where so many were killed by local peasants that only a fragment of the French force got back to Provence.

## S. Egideo (1416)

Two rival philosophies dominated the tactical concepts of the early 15th century in Italy: the Bracceschi, which supposedly emphasised the flexible use of small detachments and encouraged initiative among junior leaders, and the Sforzeschi, which supposedly concentrated on the use of massed forces and the timing of all-out assaults. Nevertheless, the victory in which the father of one of these schools, Bracchio da Montone, finally won control over his own native city was most

An early 15th century fresco commemorating the Venetian defeat of the Emperor Barbarossa off Punta Salvore, over two hundred years earlier. This painting by Spinello Aretino in the Palazzo Pubblico, Siena, illustrates the career of Pope Alexander III, a native of the city; in the usual medieval manner it depicts war-gear of the artist's own day.

The Castello Estense in the centre of Ferrara was built in 1383. Being sited on flat, low-lying ground it employed a regular plan with rectangular corner towers and a water-filled moat. Brick rather than stone was also characteristic of the broad alluvial Po Valley.

be hot he ensured that his camp was filled with jars of water sufficient for both men and horses. Bracchio now took the initiative, sending forward selected units to harry his static foe. These units then retired, reformed and if necessary refreshed themselves while others moved forward. This went on for seven hours. Perhaps the solid Malatesta ranks failed to attack their fragmented enemy because their commander still hoped to lure all of Bracchio's army into his trap. If so, he left it too late. Malatesta's troops, tortured by heat and dust in their armour, began drifting in ones and twos down to the river to drink. Soon others were breaking away in scores and although many probably returned to their positions, this unco-ordinated wandering led to considerable disarray. Bracchio now ordered a general assault which completely broke the exhausted foe. Casualties were light, but a large part of the relieving army was captured, including Carlo Malatesta himself.

## Maclodio (1427)

Francesco Bussone Carmagnola was one of the most highly paid condottieri of his day. In 1427 he was fighting for Venice, but had recently suffered a serious injury, and was no longer young. The most interesting, and unanswerable, question about his victory at Maclodio was whether Carmagnola played up these weaknesses to make his foes over-confident. The previous year Brescia had been captured from the Milanese by Carmagnola's subordinate, and during the summer of 1427 he himself led the Venetian army in a series of marches, skirmishes and the building of entrenched camps. Meanwhile the Milanese commander, Carlo Malatesta, and his two young subordinates Francesco Sforza and Niccolo Piccinino failed to bring him to battle. The Venetian government was also getting impatient; when Carmagnola wished to retire into winter quarters in September, they angrily ordered him out again.

Then, quite suddenly, the Venetian army advanced from Brescia towards the Milanese entrenched camp at Maclodio. Since this lay 15 kilometres down the Roman road towards Lodi, and as Carmagnola was able to get his men into well-concealed ambush positions by the morning

notable for another aspect of generalship. The battle of S. Egideo came about because Bracchio, a Perugian condottiere, took advantage of a lapse in Papal authority over the Papal States to attack Perugia. Having been given Bologna by a now deposed Pope, he sold that city to its own citizens and used its price of 82,000 florins to enlarge his own following of mercenaries. The Perugians, however, not only put up an effective resistance but paid another condottiere, Carlo Malatesta, to march to their relief with 5,000 men. Bracchio and Malatesta met on 15 July 1416 outside the hamlet of S. Egideo, near where the road from Perugia to Assisi crossed the River Tiber. Neither had a large army, and the battle seems to have been a pre-arranged affair.

Malatesta, as a follower of the Sforzeschi school, drew up his troops in a wide semicircle between the Tiber and the hills, hoping to lure Bracchio into an impetuous attack and surround him. Malatesta then retired to his tent to await the outcome. Bracchio, however, foresaw a long day's skirmishing and as the weather was going to of 11 October, he must have led his men on a night march. Concealment was increased by thick morning mist rising from the damp fields and irrigation systems of the region. Such fog would also have muffled sound. Maclodio was one of numerous tiny hamlets on a wide, intensively cultivated, plain that spread from the River Oglio towards Brescia. Apart from a maze of irrigation ditches, small fields, winding streams and avenues of trees or hedges, the only nearby physical feature was Monte Netto, a low isolated hill eight kilometres to the east. Roads and tracks, including the Roman road, were mostly raised on causeways above the fields which, in October, were already damp and swampy. Any rapid movement of troops would be limited to these raised causeways.

Carmagnola obviously knew the ground, for he placed most of his troops in prepared ambush positions along the Roman road and other passages leading north-east from Maclodio. A large force of 2,000 men under Niccolo da Tolentino was also hidden, probably at some distance from the road, to cut the enemy's retreat. Carmagnola then led the rest of his men in an intentionally feeble attack on the Milanese camp. Whether or not this assault surprised the enemy, their commanders were delighted to get to grips with the aged Venetian, particularly as his attack appeared so half-hearted. Malatesta ordered a counter-attack and both Sforza and Piccinino led their heavily armoured cavalry down the causeways into the autumn mist. Carmagnola withdrew, and as the Milanese advanced the Venetian ambush forces created havoc among their crowded squadrons. Some siege-crossbows mounted in threes on frames and set to shoot in a limited arc down the straight causeways caused particular damage. But in the event casualties were relatively light. As soon as Niccolo da Tolentino closed the road behind them the Milanese had little choice but to surrender, and within a very short time Carmagnola took 10,000 prisoners.

The abundance of captured banners and equipment proved an embarrassment even to the victors. Nevertheless, the allied Venetian and Florentine governments were very annoyed to learn that Sforza and Piccinino were released the following day. Malatesta soon followed, without a ransom demand, and almost all the other prisoners went home within a week, for the simple reason that Carmagnola had neither the food to feed them nor the guards to guard them. All enemy military equipment was, of course, seized, but Milan's famous arms industry enabled it to resupply its returning army almost immediately. Two of the larger armourer's workshops did, in fact, re-equip 4,000 cavalry and 2,000 infantry from their stores alone.

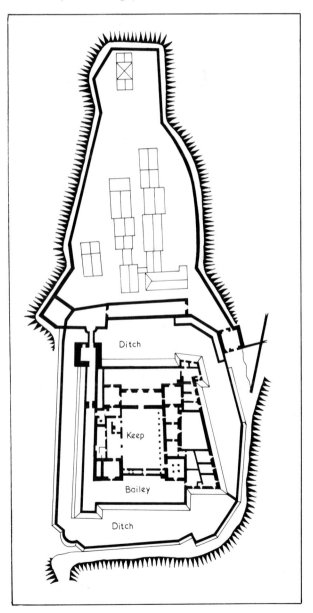

**The keep of the castle of Torrechiara is similar to those of Mantua and Ferrara in its basic plan, despite being built in a mountainous region. Its outworks are, however, completely different. Torrechiara was built for Pier Maria Rossi between 1448 and 1460 and is the finest castle in the province of Parma. (After Caciagli)**

Ditch

Keep

Bailey

Ditch

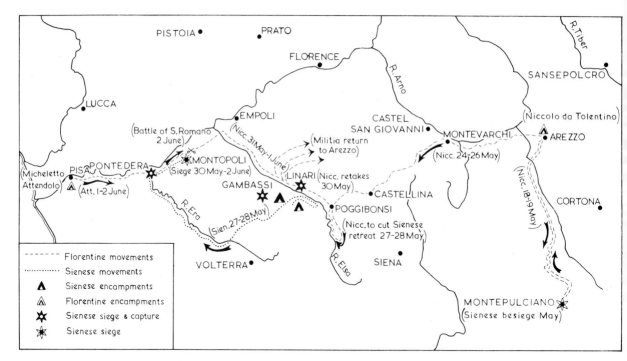

The Campaign of San Romano, 1432.

## S. Romano (1432)

The Rout of San Romano has been immortalised by Uccello's famous paintings, but it was the large-scale manoeuvring that preceded this Florentine victory that made it most interesting. Florence and Siena were once again at war. Niccolo da Tolentino, the Florentine Captain-General, was encamped near Arezzo while Micheletto Attendolo commanded a second Florentine force near Pisa. The Sienese were on the offensive, besieging the frontier fortress of Montepulciano and, aided by allied Milanese contingents, raiding the regions south of the River Arno from bases in the Elsa valley. Tolentino and 700 troops had tried to catch the Sienese commander, Francesco Piccinino, in a night ambush on 18 May but, failing to do so, had ridden south to deliver desperately needed supplies to Montepulciano. When news came that the Sienese were also close to capturing Linari and Gambassi, Tolentino decided to move fast. After three days spent collecting munitions, provisions and militia forces from the Arezzo area, he moved off at dawn on 24 May. About half of his 4,000 men were infantry, which slowed him down. News then came that Linari had fallen. On the 26th the Florentines reached Poggibonsi, where Tolentino

heard that the two Sienese forces in the Elsa valley had joined to take Gambassi and were now moving his way, towards Siena. Next day Tolentino sent infantry and militia to besiege Linari, while he himself marched south to cut off the Sienese road home. Whether or not they had been retreating, the Sienese were next reported heading north-west towards Pontedera. Sienese-held Linari and Gambassi now lay between Tolentino and his foe. Despite a lack of heavy artillery, the Florentine Captain-General determined to retake Linari rather than leave it as a threat to his rear.

The siege of 30 May was short and bitter, with heavy casualties. Linari was then razed to make it useless to an enemy while Tolentino led a forced march down the Elsa valley towards the Arno. Now he lost most of his Arezzine militia, who were getting too far from their homes and who had seen enough fighting. Although 1 June was a Sunday, normally a day of rest in Italian condottiere warfare, Tolentino would allow his men no repite when they reached the Arno. Instead they moved rapidly west towards the Sienese who, having taken Pontedera, were now besieging Montopoli from their camp at S. Romano. The Captain-General made a personal reconnaissance of the enemy's positions and then ordered an immediate attack. Presumably Tolentino had been in regular communication with Attendolo while this second, smaller, Florentine force had probably been shadowing the Sienese ever since they reached the Arno. The battle of S. Romano was short but hard-fought, with the infantry playing a vital role. Attacked first by Tolentino and then by Attendolo from the opposite side, the Sienese were completely routed.

## Fornovo (1495)

The battle of Fornovo was not the first time that an Italian condottieri army had faced an external foe. It was, however, a particularly big and savage affair between forces that no longer bore any relationship to their medieval predecessors. The French invasion of Italy in 1494 involved about 30,000 men, half cavalry and half infantry, and was resisted by Naples, the Papacy and Florence. At first it was half-heartedly supported by the Milanese, while the Venetians remained neutral. The French had heavier and more mobile artillery but their field army was steadily reduced by having to provide numerous garrisons. An unexpected invasion route, superior strategy and ruthless terror-tactics enabled Charles VIII of France successfully to march down Italy, where political indecision and a lack of inter-state co-operation, plus a collapse of civilian morale, helped him take both Rome and Naples. But in May 1495 increasing resistance and growing co-operation between the Italian states forced Charles VIII to lead the core of his army home. Instead of allowing these 10,000 Frenchmen to retreat unmolested, Francesco Gonzaga, the Venetian Captain-General who now commanded the Italian allies, tried to crush them as they came over the Apennine passes. As the invaders were retracing their route of the previous year, they marched north from the Mediterranean coast, over the Cisa Pass and down the Taro valley towards Parma. This valley widens just below Fornovo; and it was here that Gonzaga's 25,000-strong allied army of Milanese and Venetian contingents set up camp. This force consisted of 11,000 heavy cavalry, 2,000 light cavalry (mostly the Venetians' Albanian *stradiotti*), 8,000 professional infantry and a contingent of Venetian militia. The French

had 4,500 heavy cavalry, 3,000 Swiss infantry, 600 Gascon archers and 1,000 artillerymen. North of Fornovo the road beside the Taro ran along the west bank of the river, while Gonzaga's camp lay on the eastern side. Nevertheless, the French adopted a formation that anticipated resistance from the front. In true condottiere fashion, however, Gonzaga planned to strike his enemy in the flank. This meant attacking across the largely dry bed of the Taro. The Italian plan was drawn up by Gonzaga's uncle, Ridolfo, a veteran of the Franco-Burgundian wars who had wide experience of French tactics. He intended to halt the enemy's march by sending Milanese cavalry and infantry under the Count of Caiazzo against the French van. Gonzaga would attack the flank of the enemy's centre and separate it from the van, while Bernadino Fortebraccio and the Venetian cavalry did the same to the French rearguard. Venetian infantry would support Gonzaga and Fortebraccio. Meanwhile more than half the total Italian army, including the so-called Colleoneschi

**The Battle of Fornovo, 1495. (After Mallett)**

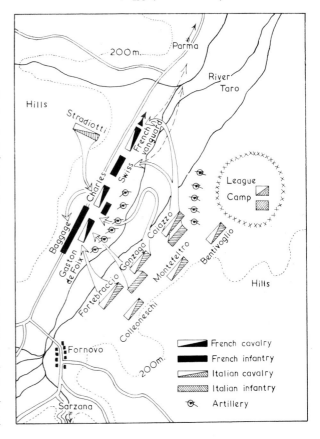

| | |
|---|---|
| ▬ | French cavalry |
| ■ | French infantry |
| ▭ | Italian cavalry |
| ▨ | Italian infantry |
| ⊛ | Artillery |

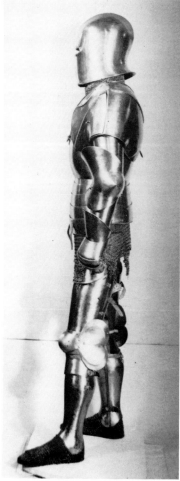

**A Milanese armour and barbuta helmet made in the Missaglia workshops for the Matsch family around 1450. (Formerly in Churburg, Alto Adige, now in the Scott Coll., reg no '39–65e, Glasgow Museums and Art Galleries)**

and a column under Antonio da Montefeltro, were to remain in reserve and only attack if personally ordered to do so by Ridolfo Gonzaga. For their part, the ferocious *stradiotti* were to sweep down from the western hills and attack the enemy's opposite flank.

The battle began in mid-afternoon with a brief artillery duel, but recent rain had so dampened both forces that their guns were largely ineffective. Worse still, these rains had caused the River Taro suddenly to rise. When Gonzaga signalled the attack, Caiazzo's Milanese moved against the French van, but the infantry, outnumbered by the Swiss, were driven off northwards. The Milanese cavalry did, however, keep the vanguard fully occupied. The *stradiotti* hit the French left, but

then lost two of their commanders, and went off to plunder the enemy's baggage train. Gonzaga's men could not cross the swollen Taro at their allotted place and so moved upstream, where they got tangled up with Fortebraccio's troops. This caused Gonzaga to strike the French line between its centre and rearguard. He thus isolated the two enemy divisions, but also had his own flank exposed to the French centre. For an hour the fighting was very intense, but the delays in crossing the river robbed the Italians of the surprise they hoped for. Worst of all, perhaps, the reserves failed to come forward because Ridolfo Gonzaga was killed at the height of the battle. At one point Charles VIII was almost captured, but such ferocious fighting could not last long and as the afternoon wore on both sides drew back to regroup. Evening then fell before battle was rejoined. Both sides claimed victory. The Italians remained masters of the field and captured the enemy's baggage, including that of the French king. But the enemy were still able to continue their march northwards while Gonzaga's army also suffered heavier losses.

# *The Plates*

## A: *The First Condottieri*

### A1: *Central Italian horseman, early 14th century*

Italian heraldry, armour and its decoration were often different from those of northern Europe in the early 14th century. This probably reflected Italy's close contacts with Byzantium and the eastern Mediterranean. Our horseman wears richly decorated *cuir-bouilli* (hardened leather) greaves, arm-defences and *cuirie* or cuirass. Note also his early form of visored helm. (Effigies, 1300–25, Salerno and Lucera Cathedrals; frescoes, *c.*1290–1300, San Gimignano; bas-relief, 1320–25, Bargello, Florence.)

### A2: *German knight, early 14th century*

German armour may have been cruder than Italian armour early in the 14th century, but it was technologically just as advanced. This knight is equipped to fight on foot. He carries an old-fashioned barrel helm, and wears a poncho-style coat-of-plates: here small flat pieces of iron were riveted inside a thick fabric garment which was buckled at the back. (Statue of St. Maurice, *c.*1300, Magdeburg Cathedral; helmet from Bozen, Castel S. Angelo, Rome.)

### A3: *Catalan man-at-arms, early 14th century*

While Spanish tactics were often considered old-fashioned, northern Spain closely followed most European technological developments. This foot-soldier, however, still carries his sword on a baldric, reflecting Moorish influence. His shield, with its pattern of nails, is of a type popular throughout the western Mediterranean. (Carving of 'Vilardell and the Dragon', *c.*1330, Barcelona Cathedral; 'Great Conquests beyond the Seas', Castilian manuscript, early 14th century, Bib. Nac. Ms.195, Madrid; Sword of Sancho IV, late 13th century, Toledo Cathedral.)

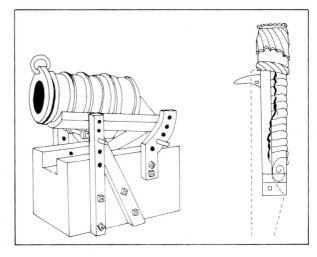

LEFT **Bombard cannon, probably Italian from the first half of the 14th century. The carriage is a modern reproduction based on a 'pezza cavalca'—'riding piece'—shown in a Milanese book entitled** *Pratica Manuale dell' Artiglieria.* **(Armoury of the Knights of St. John, Valetta).** RIGHT **Hand-cannon from a castle near Ancona, partially burst and lacking its wooden stock. It is probably Italian, of the 15th century. The breech unscrews, while the projecting hook may have been placed over a wall to absorb the recoil. (Private Collection)**

The Fortezza di Sarzanello is a well preserved example of one of the first defences built to withstand gunpowder artillery. The keep was built around 1377 while the triangular ravelin, probably the earliest still standing, was added by the Genoese in 1497, ten years after they themselves had experimented with a gunpowder-filled mine while trying to drive the Florentines from this strategic strongpoint. (After Toy)

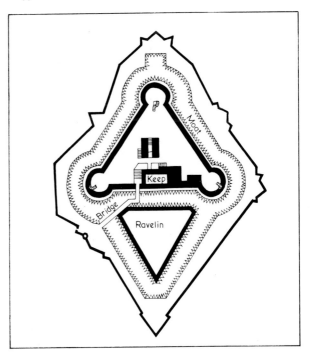

The famous equestrian statue of the condottiere Bartolomeo Colleoni, made by Verrocchio around 1480, now stands in the Campo SS. Giovanni e Paolo in Venice.

## B: The Italian Militias

### B1: North Italian infantryman, mid-14th century

Armoured men fighting with spears and large mantlet-like shields formed the core of Italian city militias. This man wears a tall visorless bascinet. Under his mail hauberk he also wears a quilted *aketon*, while from his belt hangs a large dagger known as a *basilard*. (Frescoes, c.1340, Castle of Sabbionara, Avio.)

### B2: North Italian crossbowman, mid-14th century

Crossbowmen and archers provided the offensive strength of urban militias, although it was the Italian crossbowman who was soon to earn an international reputation. This man wears a padded *aketon* and over his helmet he has an embroidered cap. At his side hang the sword and buckler (small shield) typical of most European light infantry. His crossbow is of an early wooden form, though it does now have a stirrup to make loading easier. (Frescoes, c.1340, Castle of Sabbionara, Avio.)

### B3: Venetian infantryman, first half of the 14th century

The soldiers of Venice were mostly infantry as their main task was to fight at sea as marines. This man's equipment shows the varied influences felt in Venice. His early bascinet is laced to a separate mail aventail which also has a German-style separate nasal fastened to the helmet by a turnbuckle. His extra-long triangular shield with its sharply angled corners is, by contrast, typically Byzantine. (Carved capital, early 14th century, Doge's Palace, Venice; fresco of St. Demetrius, early 14th century, Grotto of San Biagio.)

## C: The German and English Companies

### C1: Italian army commander, mid-14th century

Continuing an ancient tradition, the commander of any large force carried a baton, sometimes gilded, as his symbol of office. This nobleman is relatively lightly armoured, as was still typical of most Italian cavalry. But he does wear a coat-of-plates under his tunic. From this, chains run to his sword and dagger so that they were not lost in the heat of battle. The large epaulette-like arm protections, perhaps *espaliers*, were an Italian fashion. Some sources even show a rider being held on his horse by a heavy strap running from the cantle to the pommel of his saddle. (Carved relief of Colaccio Beccadeli, c.1340, Imola; fresco of Da Fogliano, mid-14th century, Palazzo Publico, Sienna.)

### C2: Austrian man-at-arms, mid-14th century

German military fashions, perhaps under Italian influence, became more decorative in the 14th century. This man's bascinet still has an early form of basically flat visor, while his arms are protected by splinted vambraces of a type long to remain popular in Germany. The axe was similarly still characteristic of German infantry. (Carving of 'Guards at Christ's Tomb', c.1345, Musée de l'Oeuvre Notre Dame, Strasbourg; frescoes, Castle of Sabbionara, Avio.)

### C3: English bowman, mid-14th century

This man is a veteran of the Hundred Years War and his heavy buff leather jerkin still shows the stitch marks of the Cross of St. George which identified English soldiers. His helmet is a simple structure of small metal plates sewn to a leather cap. His bow, unstrung and protected from the weather in a canvas bag, and the bracer on his left wrist are typical of a long-bow archer. For personal protection he carries a small buckler of perhaps Welsh origin and a heavy, single-edged, *falchion*. ('Luttrell Psalter', English manuscript, c.1340, British Library, London; 'Chronicle of St. Denis', French manuscript, second half of the 14th century, British Library, London; 'Walter de Milemete', English manuscript, 1326, Christ Church Lib., Oxford.)

## D: The Vipers of Milan

### D1: Lombard knight, late 14th century

Italian armour was now entering its golden age, with the work of Milanese armourers in demand throughout Europe. This knight wears a bascinet with a *hounskull* visor, while his mail aventail has a decorative cloth covering. Whereas in France armour was often worn beneath a voluminous tunic with puffed sleeves, Italians generally left their armour uncovered. Our knight has a breast-plate held in place by straps across his back, but wears no back-plate. (Milanese armour, c.1385, Churburg Castle; effigy of Jacopo Cavalli, c.1398, SS Giovanni e Paolo, Venice; chased silver altar, 1371, Pistoia Cathedral.)

### D2: North Italian hand-gunner, late 14th century

Firearms appeared early in Italy and had greater impact than elsewhere. Primitive hand-guns were important in defending the cities where such weapons, produced in large numbers, could be issued to barely trained militias. This citizen wears his town's colours and has a simple *chapel-de-fer* helmet as his only protection. (Chased silver altar, 1371, Pistoia Cathedral; fresco, 1365, Santa Maria Novella, Florence.)

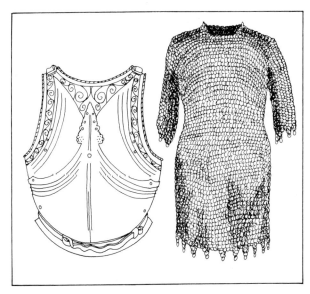

LEFT **This breastplate, which originally belonged to Bartolomeo Colleoni, dates from the mid-15th century and is in the Gothic style despite having been made in Italy. (Waffensammlung, Vienna)** RIGHT **Mail shirt from Sinigaglia near Bologna. Its rings are mixed, some whole, some riveted, and are very large. This suggests an early 14th century date, although the vandyked lower border suggests a later fashion. (Royal Scottish Museum, Edinburgh)**

### D3: Italian heavy infantry, late 14th century

Professional foot-soldiers were a vital and well-equipped element in Italian condottieri armies. This man wields a glaive, a traditional weapon in Italy, and wears a south German bascinet with a *klappvisier* hinged at the brow. His body armour is probably of *cuir-bouilli* hardened leather, plus smaller metal plates, riveted to a decorative velvet covering. ('Battle of Clavigo', fresco, c.1370, Oratorio di S. Giorgio, Padua, 'Gallic Wars', Italian manuscript, c.1390, Trivulzian Lib., Milan.)

## E: Bracceschi and Sforzeschi

### E1: Italian knight, c.1425

The 15th century was the true Age of Plate in the history of armour. This horseman need not have been a nobleman as many leading condottieri had humble origins. He is, however, clearly rich for he wears a Milanese armour of the finest quality. To this would be added an *armet* type of helmet. His spurs are very long, as was necessary when riding in a tall 'peaked' saddle. His dagger is of the *rondel* style. (Milanese armour, c.1425, Churburg Castle; effigy of an Italian knight, early 15th century, Louvre, Paris; 'Annunciation', fresco by Pisanello, c.1425, San Fermo, Verona.)

### E2: Italian light infantry, first half of the 15th century

The role of light infantry was vital in those sieges that dominated Italian Renaissance warfare. This man wears a velvet-covered sallet and carries the large wooden shield that became characteristic of Italy's infantry. Apart from a padded *aketon* his only armour is a leg harness worn on the vulnerable left leg, which was normally advanced forward when fighting in ranks. ('Rout of San Romano', by Uccello, *c.*1455, Uffizi Gallery, Florence; 'Camp scene', Veronese manuscript drawing, early 15th century, British Museum, London.)

### E3: Artilleryman, early 15th century

Bombards (in the background) and other forms of cannon were widely used in Italy. At first they were mounted on frames without wheels. This gunner carries a stone cannon-ball and has a *touch* thrust into his belt. This was an iron rod to be heated in a brazier and then used to fire the gun. He also wears a late 14th century bascinet, modified and with its visor removed. (Italian bombard, early 15th century, Artillery Museum, Turin; modified Italian bascinet, *c.*1400, Wallace Collection, London.)

### F: Malatesta and Montefeltro

### F1: North Italian light cavalrymen, c.1460

Fifteenth century Italian light cavalry were quite heavily armoured by earlier standards. This man wears a *barbuta*, a form of sallet that gave good protection while not restricting its wearer's breathing. His armour also lacks the heavy *pauldrons* that tended to restrict arm movement. Note the lance-rest on his breastplate. (Milanese armour made for Frederick I, *c.*1450, Waffensammlung, Vienna; Milanese armour made for Ulrich IX, *c.*1445, Churburg Castle; Milanese sallet, *c.*1450, Scott Coll., Glasgow; fresco from Sabbionara, mid-15th century, Diocesan Museum, Trento.)

### F2: Italian knight, c.1460

This horseman wears the full equipment designed for jousting with the lance. The large crest on his helmet would normally have been reserved for tournaments or parades, while the large *pauldrons* on his shoulders completed his overall protection.

The condottieri leader Niccolò da Tolentino defeating the Sienese in 1432 at the Rout of San Romano. This painting, made by Uccello between 1450 and 1459, illustrates the equipment of that date rather than of the year of the battle itself. (National Gallery, inv. 583, London)

His horse's armour consists of a head-protecting *chamfron*, a scale *crinet* and a rigid iron *barde* beneath a heraldic *caparison*. Such defences made the animal slow but almost as impervious to attack as its rider. ('Rout of San Romano', by Uccello, *c.* 1460, National Gallery, London; Milanese armour, *c.*1440–60, Scott Coll., Glasgow; Florentine *cassone* chest, *c.*1450–70, National Gallery, Dublin; Milanese horse-armour, *c.*1450, City of Vienna Historical Museum; portrait of Federigo de Montefeltro by Della Francesca, *c.*1470, Brera Gallery, Milan.)

*: Venice and the North*

*1 : Sienese crossbowman, late 15th century*
Crossbowmen were now the most effective infantry
in most European armies and those of the Italian
city-states were justifiably famous. Lightly armoured and relying on heavy wooden *pavise*
mantlets (shields propped up on stays) for protection, these troops used increasingly powerful
crossbows. They were still more accurate than
hand-guns but were also more expensive. This
man loads his steel-bowed weapon with a detach-
able windlass. He also wears an Italian sallet and
carries a Venetian sword from the close of the
15th century. ('Siege of Perugia', by Benedetto
Bonfiglio, *c.*1455–70, Galeria Nazionale, Perugia;
Italian helmet from Rhodes, 1457–1500, Tower

of London; Venetian sword, late 15th century,
Met. Museum, New York.)

*G2 : Venetian colonial archer, late 15th century*
Venice ruled an empire of islands and coastal
towns scattered across the eastern Mediterranean,
so oriental influences were naturally seen in much
Venetian military equipment. This archer wears
a sallet which has one side hinged so that he does
not snag his bowstring. His recurve bow is of a
composite Turkish or Balkan type. His quiver is
also very Turkish, whereas his sword is a *spada alla
stradiotta*. Such weapons in the Stradiot, or
'colonial soldier', fashion were popular among
Venetian naval troops. (Italian archer's sallet,
*c.*1470, Wallace Coll., London; 'Life of St.

'St. Michael' by Perugino, c. 1500. This painting forms the left wing of a triptych of the Madonna and Child. It portrays fine Italian armour of the late 15th century, although the saint's shield is entirely fanciful. (National Gallery, inv. 288, London)

Ursula', by Carpacchio, 1490–93, Acad. Gallery, Venice; Venetian sword, c.1500, Bargello, Florence; Pisanello's pencil sketches of the Byzantine Emperor's retinue, mid-15th century, Chicago Art Institute.)

## G3: Venetian heavy infantryman, late 15th century

Heavily armoured soldiers had a vital role, both at sea and on the land, in the armies of Venice. This man's equipment is strictly European, though the turban round his helmet probably reflects current Venetian orientalized fashions. His helmet is also unusual in having a long curved nasal. He carries a typically large infantry shield and wields a long-hafted war-hammer designed to penetrate armour. He also wears a *brigandine*, a very flexible version of the coat-of-plates, over his mail hauberk. ('Life of St. Ursula', by Carpaccio, 1490–93, Acad. Gallery, Venice.)

## H: The Invasion of Italy

### H1: Spanish man-at-arms, end of the 15th century

The heavily armed infantrymen of Spain were to become the most feared and effective troops in Europe. Their tactics had been perfected in wars that united Spain and their equipment was often heavier than that of Spain's famous light cavalry who fought *à la jineta* in Moorish style. This reversed the normal European practice where heavy cavalry were supported by lighter infantry. He wears a *cabacete* helmet and a *barbote* rigid neck-guard. His weapon is a pole-axe designed to combat cavalry. (Monument of Infante Alfonso, c.1490, Cartuja de Miraflores, Burgos; Spanish helmet and barbote, late 15th century, Pauillac Coll., Paris; Spanish armour c.1500(?), Musée de l'Armée, Paris.)

### H2: Italian knight, end of the 15th century

This period saw what many regard as the peak of Italian armour design. Unlike the best German armours, with their almost barbaric abundance of decoration, late 15th and early 16th century Italian armours were as stark and functional as a modern warplane. Note the scientifically shaped gauntlets protecting his wrists, the large *couters* with their different shapes to protect the elbows of his left (bridle) and right (sword) arms, plus the large *gardbrace* with its vertical *haute-piece* covering his left shoulder and neck. (Armour from the Sanctuary of Madonna delle Grazie, Ducal Palace, Mantua; 'St Florian', by Zaganelli, 1499, Brera Gallery, Milan; 'Warrior', by Vivarini, c.1480, Uffizi, Florence.)

## H3: French hand-gunner, end of the 15th century

By now hand-guns had grown more powerful and accurate. The *arquebus*, for example, was fired by a reliable match-lock trigger system. The gunners of France developed their skills in the successful final phases of the Hundred Years War against England. This soldier wears a sallet with circular ear-pieces, a fashion that might have had Ottoman Turkish or even Mongol origins. His short iron *plackart* is worn over a cloth-covered *brigandine*, while at his side hang a primitive powder-flask and an Italian *cinquedea* short-sword or large dagger. (Italian arquebus, late 15th century, Castel S. Angelo, Rome; 'Life of St. Sermin', French carved relief, *c*.1490, Amiens Cathedral; Italian sword, *c*.1500, Wallace Coll., London.)

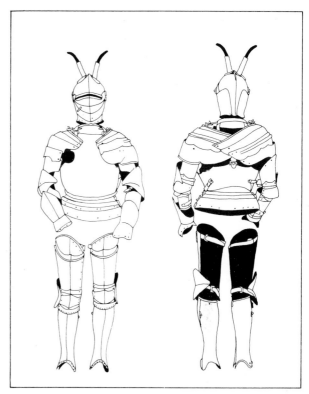

**The so-called 'Devil's Mask', an Italian armour of around 1490 with wooden horns forming a crest on the sparrow-beak armet. This armour was rediscovered in 1968 and has recently been restored in Florence. (From the church of La Madonna delle Grazie, Udine)**

**Venetian and German infantry armours of the late 15th and early 16th centuries (Stibbert Collection, Florence)**

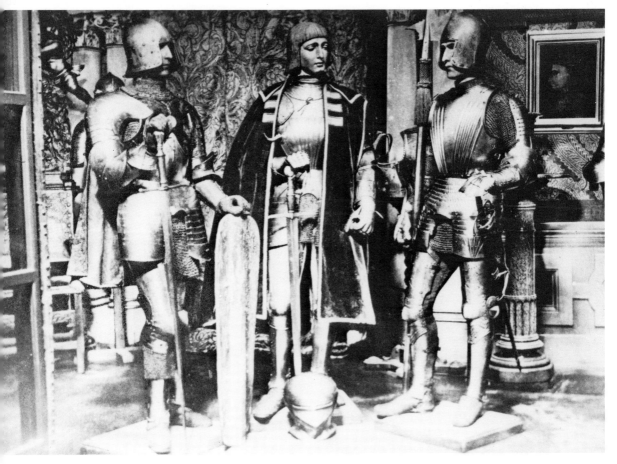

# Notes sur les planches en couleurs

**A1** Armure richement décorée, en cuir durci, dénotant des contacts étroits, antérieurement, entre l'Italie et l'empire Byzantin. Remarquer egalement une version ancienne de casque à visière. **A2** L'armure allemande était d'un style plus ancien et plus simple, mais tout aussi efficace. L'armure de corps est réalisée en plaquettes de fer rivées à l'intérieur de vêtements de tissu épais, se bouclant à l'arrière. **A3** Ce fantassin trahit l'influence mauresque dans la façon de tenir l'épée. Le bouclier décoré d'un motif à clous était en vogue dans toute la Méditérranée occidentale.

**B1** Hauberk en mailles porté sur l'aketon capitonné. Les lanciers portant de grands boucliers constituaient le coeur des milices des villes italiennes. **B2** Noter la coiffure brodée portée sur le casque. **B3** Casque bascinet avec barre nasale de type allemand, fixée à l'aventail en mailles; long bouclier triangulaire, à arêtes aiguës dans les coins, de style byzantin. Les fantassins véniciens combattaient surtout en mer.

**C1** Remarquer le bâton de commandement; chaînes attachant l'épée et la dague à la 'cote de plaquettes' portée sous la tunique. Les épaulettes décorées—espaliers—constituaient une mode italienne. **C2** Ancien style de visière; noter les défenses de bras en bandes métalliques qui demeuraient en vogue en Allemagne. **C3** Un vétéran de la Guerre de Cent Ans: il continue à arborer la marque de la Croix de St. Georges sur son justaucorps. Ce casque, peu commun, est réalisé en plaquettes de fer fixées sur un capuchon. Remarquer l'arc enveloppé et porté en bandoulière, le petit bouclier, et le 'falchion'.

**D1** Armure fine de fabrication milanaise, avec aventail revêtu de tissu; pas de contre-plaque—la plaque pectorale est sanglée derrière le torse. **D2** Les armes à feu étaient des armes importantes pour les gardes qui, avec un peu d'entraînement, devaient défendre les murs de leur ville. **D3** Fantassin de métier appartenant à une bande de condottieri, portant un casque de style allemand, une armure de corps en cuir et métal rivetée sous un revêtement en tissu; le glaive est typique des armées italiennes.

**E1** Cette armure milanaise d'excellente qualité identifie un homme riche; un casque 'armet' complèterait la tenue. **E2** Le casque revêtu de velours et l'armure de la jambe gauche, exposée dans les combats, constituent la seule protection indépendamment de l'aketon. **E3** Cet homme porte un boulet de canon en pierre et a passé dans sa ceinture la tige de fer qui, chauffée, servait à la mise à feu du canon.

**F1** Cavalerie légère: elle portait alors des armures fort lourdes. Remarquer l'absence de lourde armure d'épaule qui gênait les mouvements, et la fixation d'un support de lance sur la plaque pectorale. Le casque est le 'barbuta'. **F2** Equipement de joute, complet avec panache héraldique et armure complète pour le cheval.

**G1** Les arbalétriers italiens étaient fameux dans toute l'Europe. Remarquer le treuil pour l'arbalète et le pavise de protection; casque sallet; épée vénicienne. **G2** L'arc et le carquois témoignent de l'influence de la méditerranée orientale, commune parmi les troupes du vaste empire de Venise. **G3** Fantassin vénicien typique, lourdement équipé et portant une armure de corps souple 'brigandine'; un marteau de guerre sur un long fût. Le casque montre l'influence orientale.

**H1** Soldats de l'infanterie lourde espagnole, portant souvent des armures plus complètes que de nombreux cavaliers: ils étaient redoutés dans toute l'Europe. Le casque est du type cabacete, porté avec un couvre-nuque rigide: barbote. Le merlin était destiné à lutter contre des cavaliers. **H2** L'armure italienne remarquablement nette et fonctionnelle, avec défenses de bras asymétriques, à configuration étudiée scientifiquement pour les combats montés. **H3** L'armure de corps est un plackart en fer, porté sur une brigandine; le long couteau est un cinquedea italien, et le casque 'sallet' comporte des protecteurs d'oreilles circulaires d'un style susceptible d'avoir des origes orientales.

# Farbtafeln

**A1** Die reich verzierte Rüstung aus gehärtetem Leder spiegelt möglicherweise den engen Kontakt zwischen Italien und dem byzantinischen Reich wider. Beachten Sie dieses frühe Exemplar eines Helmes mit Visier. **A2** Diese deutsche Rüstung ist etwas älter und einfacher, aber dennoch genauso gut. Die Körperrüstung ist aus Eisenplättchen gefertigt, die in einem dicken Stoffgewand vernietet sind; das Gewand wird auf dem Rücken mit einer Schnalle verschlossen. **A3** Bei diesem Fusssoldat erkennt man den maurischen Einfluss an der Art, wie er sein Schwert trägt. Das mit Nägeln verzierte Schild war im ganzen Mittelmeerraum weit verbreitet.

**B1** Ein Ketten-Hauberk, der über gepolstertem Stoff-Aketon getragen wird. Die Stärke der italienischen Stadtmiliz lag bei diesen Speerträgern mit grossen Schildern. **B2** Beachten Sie die bestickte Kappe über dem Helm. **B3** Bascinet-Helm mit einem Ketten-Aventail befestigtem, deutschen Nasenschutz; langes dreieckiges Schild mit spitzen Ecken im byzantinischen Stil. Venizianische Fusssoldaten kämpften hauptsächlich zu Wasser als 'Marinesoldaten'.

**C1** Beachten Sie den Kommandostab; aus Sicherheitsgründen sind Schwert und Dolch am Panzerhemd unter der Tunika festgekettet. Die verzierten Schulterteile—Espaliers—waren in Italien grosse Mode. **C2** Frühe Art eines Visiers. Beachten Sie ausserdem den Armschutz in Form von Metallstreifen, der in Deutschland noch lange populär war. **C3** Ein Veteran aus dem hundertjährigen Krieg. Er hat noch das St.-Georg-Kreuz auf seinem Lederwams. Der ungewöhnliche Helm ist aus Eisenplättchen gefertigt, die an der Kappe befestigt werden. Beachten Sie den um die Schulter gehängten, eingewickelten Bogen, den runden Schild und den Falchion.

**D1** Feine Rüstung Mailänder Herstellung mit stoffüberzogenem Aventail ohne Rückenpanzer; der Brustpanzer wird hinter dem Rumpf festgeschnallt. **D2** Frühe Gewehre waren für die nahezu unausgebildete Miliz, die ihre Stadtmauern verteidigen mussten, von grösster Wichtigkeit. **D3** Berufsinfanterist einer Condottieri-Einheit mit einem Helm im deutschen Stil und einer Köperrüstung aus Leder und vernietetem Metall unter einem Stoffüberzug sowie mit dem für die italienische Armee typischen Glaive.

**E1** An der erstklassigen, Mailändischen Rüstung sieht man, dass sie einem wohlhabenden Mann gehört—zu der Ausrüstung fehlt nur noch ein Armet-Helm. **E2** Ausser einem Aketon sind der samtbezogene Helm und der rechte Beinschutz, den er im Kampf vorn behält, sein einziger Schutz. **E3** Dieser Soldat trägt eine Kanonenkugel aus Stein, in seinem Gürtel steckt der Eisenstab, der erhitzt und mit dem die Kanone gefeuert wird.

**F1** Die 'Leichte Kavallerie' war hier allerdings mit schwerer Rüstung versehen. Beachten Sie, dass kein schwerer Schulterschutz vorhanden ist, der die Bewegungsfreiheit einschränken könnte. Beachten Sie ausserdem die Lanzenauflage an seinem Brustpanzer. Der Helm ist eine Barbuta. **F2** Volle Turnierrüstung mit Familienwappen sowie voller Pferderüstung.

**G1** Italienische Armbrustschützen waren in ganz Europa bekannt. Beachten Sie die Winde zum Laden der Armbrust sowie das schützende Pavise, den Sallet-Helm und das venezianische Schwert. **G2** Bogen und Köcher bezeugen den deutlichen Einfluss aus dem Mittelmeerraum, der bei Truppen aus dem riesigen, venezianischen Reich oft zu finden ist. **G3** Typischer, venezianischer Fusssoldat in schwerer, flexibler Brigadine-Körperrüstung und einem 'Kriegshammer' an einem langen Schaft. Der Helm zeigt einen östlichen Einfluss.

**H1** Die schwere, spanische Infanterie, die oft mit stärkeren Rüstungen versehen war, als die Kavallerie, wurde in ganz Europa gefürchtet. Der cabacete-artige Helm wurde mit dem steifen Barbote-Halsschutz getragen, die Streitaxt war für den Kampf gegen die Kavallerie vorgesehen. **H2** Der Höhepunkt der italienischen Rüstungen: sauber und praktisch mit exakt geformtem, asymmetrischem Armschutz für den Kampf zu Pferde. **H3** Diese Körperrüstung besteht aus einem Eisen-Plackart, der über einer Brigadine getragen wird. Das lange Messer ist eine italienische Cinquedea und der Sallet-Helm verfügt über einen runden Ohrschutz, der seinen Ursprung möglicherweise im Orient hat.